Pleasing Polish Recipes

Edited by Jacek and Malgorzata Nowakowski, Michelle
Miriam Canter, Hannelore Bozeman, John Zug, and Joa
Drawings by Alice Wadowski-Bak.
Pisanki on cover are from the collection of Rev. Czesła
Polish Civic Coats of Arms.

CZĘSTOCHOWA

GDAŃSK

KRAKOW

BOOKS BY MAIL Stocking Stuffers POSTPAID You may mix titles. One book for $9.95; two for $16; three for $23; four for $28; twelve for $75. (*Prices subject to change.*) Please call 1-800-728-9998

American Gothic Cookbook
Cherished Czech Recipes
Czech & Kolache Recipes
   & Sweet Treats
Dandy Dutch Recipes
Dear Danish Recipes
Fine Finnish Foods
Great German Recipes
License to Cook Italian Style
Norwegian Recipes
Pleasing Polish Recipes **(this book)**
Quality Czech Mushroom Recipes
Quality Dumpling Recipes
Recipes from Ireland
Savory Scottish Recipes

Scandinavian Holiday Recipes
Scandinavian Smorgasbord Recipes
Scandinavian Style Fish and Seafood Recipes
Scandinavian Sweet Treats
Slavic Specialties
Splendid Swedish Recipes
Ukrainian Recipes
License to Cook Arizona Style
License to Cook Iowa Style
License to Cook Kansas Style
License to Cook Minnesota Style
License to Cook New Mexico Style
License to Cook Texas Style
License to Cook Wisconsin Style
Waffles, Flapjacks, Pancakes (Scandinavia & Around the World.)

PENFIELD PRESS • 215 BROWN STREET • IOWA CITY, IA 52245-5842

Contents

GNIEZNO

Christianity Comes to Poland

The sgrafitto mural, left, at St. Francis High School Faculty House, Athol Springs, New York, shows Christianity coming to Poland when the ruler, Mieszko, was baptized in 966. Poles and Polish Americans rejoiced when Karol Cardinal Wojtyła of Poland became Pope John Paul II in 1978.

4

Polish Americans

Being a Polish American means to me: To be proud of the American heritage; to be familiar with achievements of both nations; of their goals and traditions.

To be part of the mainstream of American life, to have the privilege of serving both countries all the way.

To be a good Catholic and to promote Polish culture among the Americans.

Andrew Azarjew, Editor, Narod Polski, Chicago, Illinois

More than 11 million Americans belong to one or more of the 10,000 Polish-American organizations. Additional millions of Americans claim Polish roots. Poles have been coming here since before the American Revolution.

The great immigration of more than two million Poles took place from 1880 to World War I. More came after World War II as refugees, as did another wave fleeing Communist Poland's outlawing of Solidarity in the 1980s. The greatest concentration of Polish Americans are found in Illinois, Michigan, Ohio, New York, New Jersey, Pennsylvania, and Indiana.

The first mass migration of Poles to America was to Panna Maria, Texas, in 1854 under the leadership of Rev. Leopold Moczygemba, Conventual Franciscan. Father Moczygemba is shown in this mural by Professor Jozef Slawinski at St. Francis High School, Faculty House, Athol Springs, New York.

Sites to See

The Polish Museum of America, sponsored by the Polish Roman Catholic Union of America, Chicago, Illinois.

The Copernicus Cultural and Civic Center, Chicago, Illinois.

The Polish Museum, Winona, Minnesota.

Polish businesses in Chicago, Illinois, Buffalo, New York, and Hamtramck, Michigan.

The Buffalo City Market, Buffalo, New York.

Orchard Lake Schools (St. Mary's College, Saint Mary's Preparatory and SS. Cyril & Methodius Seminary), Orchard Lake, Michigan.

Panna Maria, Texas.

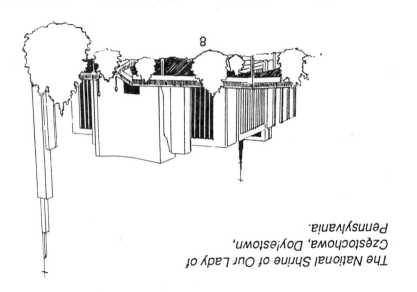

8

*The National Shrine of Our Lady of
Czestochowa, Doylestown,
Pennsylvania.*

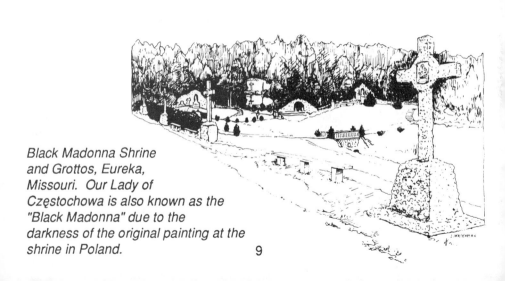

Black Madonna Shrine and Grottos, Eureka, Missouri. Our Lady of Częstochowa is also known as the "Black Madonna" due to the darkness of the original painting at the shrine in Poland.

9

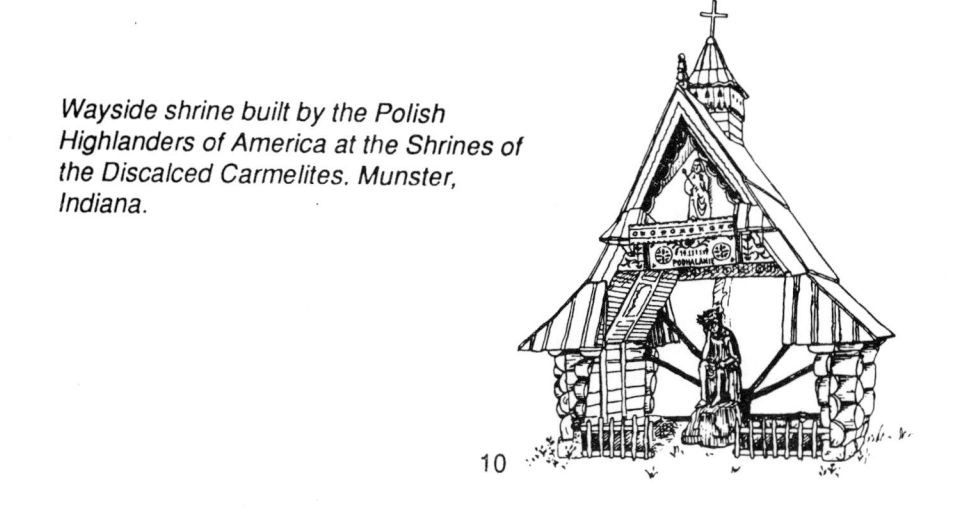

Wayside shrine built by the Polish Highlanders of America at the Shrines of the Discalced Carmelites. Munster, Indiana.

10

The Royal Sleigh. Polish Museum of America, Chicago, Illinois.
This one-horse open sleigh, carved from a single log in 1703, was a Christmas present from Polish King Stanislaw Leszczynski to his daughter Princess Maria, a future wife of Louis XV of France. (Gift of the John D. and Catherine T. MacArthur Foundation.)

11

Woodcarving at the Polish Highlanders of America Club, Chicago, Illinois, where there is a full-service restaurant and bar.

The sgrafitto mural at St. Francis High School, Faculty House, Athol Springs, New York depicts Fr. Justin Figas, OFM Conv., at right, who originated the Rosary Hour radio network program in 1931 at Corpus Christi Church, Buffalo, New York. Fr. Cornelian Dende, OFM Conv., is heard now on the Father Justin Rosary Hour throughout the United States and Canada. At the top is a representation of Our Lady of Częstochowa, Queen of Poland, a venerated painting at Jasna Góra in Poland.

"Polish Szopka" © *Alice Wadowski-Bak*

Polish Szopka by © Alice Wadowski-Bak, Niagara Falls, New York. The szopka (puppet show) is a Polish tradition dating back to the medieval era. These szopki often resemble the famous St. Mary's Church in Kraków. The nativity scene or crèche is on the first floor. Teen-age boys carry the szopki from house to house singing carols along the way.

14

Dyeing Traditional Brown Easter Eggs

1 dozen eggs
skins of 5 pounds of onions with
    colored skins
1 tablespoon salt
water
bacon fat or oil

Place eggs, onion skins, and salt in a large pot. Cover with water and bring to a slow boil so the eggs do not crack. Boil 5 minutes. Remove eggs and let them cool. You will have clay-brown eggs. To give them a shine, wipe with bacon fat or oil. **Note:** Tea will also color eggs brown.

Traditional Pisanki

15

Polish Table Grace

*Pobłogosław Panie Boże nas, pobłogosław ten
posiłek, tych którzy go przygotowali i
naucz nas dzielić się chlebem i radością
ze wszystkimi. Przez Chrystusa Pana naszego. Amen.*

*Plate Featuring
Pope John Paul II*

Bless us, O Lord, bless this food, bless those
who prepared it and teach us to share our
bread and joy with others. Through Christ our Lord.
Amen.

*Fr. Cornelian Dende, OFM Conv.,
Director of the Father Justin Rosary Hour,
Athol Springs, New York*

Appetizers & Beverages

Deviled Eggs with Mushroom Bits	20
Eggs "in the Shell"	19
Hot Beer	22
Iced Coffee Polish Style	21
Juniper Vodka	25
Mead	23
Steak Tartare	18
Stuffed Goose Necks	26

Opoczno Region

Steak Tartare

1 pound ground sirloin steak
2 onions, chopped
2 egg yolks

1 tablespoon vegetable oil
juice of 1/2 lemon
1 tablespoon Dijon mustard
salt and pepper to taste

Mix all ingredients together. Serve immediately with bread and butter. Serves 4.

Wycinanki *by Alice Wadowski-Bak*

18

Eggs "in the Shell"

8 hard-cooked eggs, shells intact
4 tablespoons butter, softened
salt and pepper to taste

1 1/2 tablespoons fresh chopped dill
1/2 cup grated cheese
paprika

Slice the eggs lengthwise. Scoop out the egg, reserving the shells. Chop the eggs and add the remaining ingredients, except the paprika. Mix well. Spoon the egg mixture into the shells and sprinkle with paprika. Broil the eggs until browned. Serves 8.

Deviled Eggs with Mushroom Bits

8 hard-cooked eggs, peeled and halved
salt
5 tablespoons mayonnaise

3/4 teaspoon dry mustard
1/4 cup chopped mushrooms
1 teaspoon butter
paprika, optional

Remove yolks from eggs and place in a bowl; mash until no lumps remain. Add salt, mayonnaise, and mustard. Sauté mushrooms in butter. Add to egg yolk mixture. Fill the egg whites with the yolk mixture. Serve dusted with paprika.

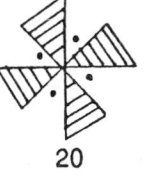

20

Iced Coffee Polish Style

1/2 cup sugar
5 cups strong coffee

1 cup vanilla ice cream
3/4 cup vodka
2 cups whipped cream for topping

Combine sugar and coffee. Chill several hours. Place 1/4 cup ice cream in each of 4 serving glasses. Add 1 1/2 ounce vodka to each glass. Divide the coffee mixture among the cups and serve topped with whipped cream.

21

Hot Beer

4 cups beer
1 cinnamon stick
6 cloves

6 egg yolks
1/3 cup sugar

In a medium-sized saucepan, combine beer, cinnamon, and cloves. Cover and bring to a boil. Remove cinnamon and cloves from beer. Cream eggs and sugar. Beating constantly to prevent curdling, slowly add hot beer to egg mixture; continue beating until frothy. Serves 4 to 6.

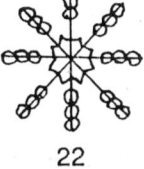

Mead

1 quart strained honey
3 quarts water
nutmeg
pieces of ginger

piece of dried orange peel
1 teaspoon hops
1 teaspoon juniper berries
1 1/2 ounces fresh yeast

Cook honey with the water for 1 hour. Place nutmeg, ginger, orange peel, hops, and juniper berries in a piece of cheesecloth, tie it closed, secure a weight on the end and place in honey mixture. Boil another hour. Cool honey and place in a carboy, an airtight container that will allow gases to escape but will not allow air to enter; these can be found at wine- and beer-making shops.

(continued)

Mead   *(continued)*

Dissolve the yeast in a little of the honey mixture, then add to the mead. Seal carboy. Mead will ferment at room temperature for 6 months. When the mead is fermented the carboy will stop bubbling. Place carboy in a cool dry place. After a year the mead will definitely be through fermenting and you can transfer it to bottles and seal the tops. Watch for delayed fermentation and if observed, open the bottle to allow the fermentation to finish, then close again. If fermentation occurs in a sealed bottle, the container will most likely blow up. The longer the mead sits the better it gets.

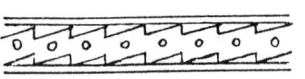

Juniper Vodka

1/2 cup juniper berries, crushed
1 quart grain alcohol

2 cups water, divided
1 pound sugar

Soak crushed juniper berries in alcohol and 1 cup of the water for a week. Boil sugar and remaining water until syrupy. Strain juniper alcohol through blotting paper or other filter. Add to sugar mixture. Set aside for a few months to ferment. The outcome is similar to gin but stronger.

Plate from Poland featuring the White Eagle.

Stuffed Goose Necks

1 large goose neck
1 goose liver
1/2 pound ground veal
2 ounces salt pork, ground
1 tablespoon butter
2 egg yolks

1/2 cup bread crumbs
1/4 cup milk
pinch ground nutmeg
salt and pepper
4 large mushrooms, thinly sliced
2 slices bacon, cooked and crumbled
4 cups chicken broth

Remove skin from goose neck carefully, so as not to tear, reserving skin. Discard goose neck. Press liver through a fine sieve. Combine liver with remaining ingredients, except broth. Mix well. Stuff goose neck skin with this mixture. Sew up both ends of neck skin and prick all over. Heat broth to a simmer and place stuffed neck in broth. Simmer 1 hour, then remove from broth. Chill, slice, and serve cold. Serves 4.

Soups

Barley Soup	40	Pea Soup	44
Beef and Chicken Stock	32	Polish Cold Soup with Shrimp	35
Beet *Kvas*	34	Rhubarb and Strawberry Soup	45
Blueberry Soup	38	Rye Flour *Kvas*	41
Borscht	49	Savory Polish Split Pea Soup	28
Dill Pickle Soup	46	Sorrel Soup	39
Duck Blood Soup	50	Tomato Soup	31
Herring Sauce	33	Vegetable Soup	43
Lenten Borscht	29	White Borscht	42
Mushroom Soup	47	White Easter Soup	48

Savory Polish Split Pea Soup

Audrey Kowalski, Kowalski Sausage Co., Hamtramck, Michigan.

4 Polish sausages
2 teaspoons butter
2 11-ounce cans condensed
　split pea soup
11 ounces milk (1 can)

11 ounces water (1 can)
1 stalk celery, thinly sliced diagonally
1 medium-sized onion, thinly sliced
1 sprig parsley
1 bay leaf

Place sausages in cold water. Bring to a boil; simmer 10 minutes. Drain. Over low heat, pan-fry sausages in butter until browned. Remove, keep warm, save drippings. Empty pea soup into a different saucepan; add milk and water a little at a time, stirring until smooth. Sauté celery, onion, parsley, and bay leaf in sausage drippings until onion is crisp. Add to soup, blend. Place sausages on top of soup mixture. Reheat to a gentle boil. To serve sausage: remove from soup, cut into slices, divide into each serving of soup. Serves 4 to 5.

Lenten Borscht

8 medium-sized beets, peeled
6 cups water
2 ounces dried mushrooms
1 carrot, sliced
1 celery stalk, sliced
1 small parsley root, chopped
1 leek, sliced
2 onions, sliced, divided

a carp head, optional
1 teaspoon salt
salted dill, whole
1 garlic clove, crushed
1 pint beet *kvas*, recipe on page 34
1 fresh beet, ground, optional
1 teaspoon butter
salt

(continued)

Lenten Borscht *(continued)*

Boil the whole beets in water with the mushrooms and sliced vegetables except 1 sliced onion. Add the cleaned carp head, salt, salted dill and garlic. When the beets are tender, take them out; strain the liquid. Slice the beets; add the beet *kvas* and the sliced beets to the liquid. To improve the color of the borscht, add ground fresh beet. Brown the sliced onion in butter; add to the liquid. Season to taste. Bring to a boil. Serves 6 to 8.

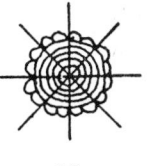

Tomato Soup

8 cups chicken or beef broth
1 large parsley root
1 carrot
1 celery stalk
1 leek
5 small sprigs parsley

1 small onion
1 can tomato paste
1/4 teaspoon flour dissolved
    in 3 tablespoons of water
salt and pepper to taste
8 teaspoons sour cream

Clean the vegetables. Combine the broth with the vegetables and cook for about 60 minutes. Cool the vegetable broth and discard the vegetables. Dissolve the tomato paste in the broth. Bring to boil and simmer for 3 minutes. Add the flour mixture, stirring in well. Serve in small bowls with 1 teaspoon of sour cream in each. It can be served with cooked rice or noodles in the soup. Serves 8.

Beef and Chicken Stock

2 pounds beef with the bone
1/2 chicken
1 large carrot
2 parsley roots
1 stalk celery
1 medium-sized leek

1 yellow onion
4 cups chopped savoy cabbage
1 bay leaf
salt to taste
thyme to taste
5 peppercorns

Cover the meat with water. Bring it to boiling. Skim off the foam. Add vegetables and spices. Continue boiling for another 30 minutes or until meat is tender. Take off the stove, cool, and remove the meat. Strain the broth and skim off the fat. Serve hot with noodles or dumplings. Perfect for a cold winter day. Serves 8.

Note: This soup can be made using all chicken or all beef. It is a soup in itself or may be used as a base for another soup.

Herring Sauce

1/2 salted herring, boneless
a piece of lemon
3 shallots
1 tablespoon vegetable oil
1 apple, peeled, cored, and
   cut into pieces

1/2 teaspoon sugar
salt and pepper
1/2 cup sour cream
1/2 cup mayonnaise

Clean the herring and discard all the bones. Put herring and all the ingredients except the sour cream and mayonnaise into a blender and blend until smooth. Mixing constantly, add sour cream and mayonnaise. Perfect as salad dressing.

Beet Kvas

6 cups boiled water, cold
3 cooked beets, sliced

3 slices whole rye bread, crumbled,
Rye Bread recipe on page 69

Pour the water over the beets. Add the crumbled whole rye bread. Let stand at room temperature for 3 to 5 days. Drain off the juice and use the clear liquid as a base for borscht.

Polish Cold Soup with Shrimp

Ronald S. Nowak, Sales Director, Polish Union of America, Buffalo, New York.

1 small bunch firm young beets,
  peeled and grated
1 1/2 quarts cold water
3 tablespoons red wine vinegar, divided
5 teaspoons salt, divided
1 1/2 teaspoons sugar, divided
1 pound uncooked shrimp
  (or crayfish tails in season)
1 quart water
1 cup sour cream

2 medium-sized cucumbers,
  seeded, and diced
4 medium-sized scallions,
  including 2 inches of the
  green tops, sliced
4 red radishes, thinly sliced
4 tablespoons finely chopped fresh dill
  leaves or 4 teaspoons dried dill weed,
  divided
3 tablespoons strained fresh lemon juice

(continued)

Polish Cold Soup with Shrimp   *(continued)*

pinch white pepper
1 lemon, thinly sliced, garnish

3 hard-cooked eggs, chilled and
 finely chopped for garnish

Bring the grated beets and cold water to a boil over high heat in a 3- to 4-quart enameled or stainless-steel saucepan. Reduce heat to moderate and cook uncovered for 1 minute. Reduce heat to low, stir in 2 tablespoons vinegar, 2 teaspoons salt and 1 teaspoon sugar; simmer, partially covered, for 30 minutes. Drain the beets. Set the beets and the cooking liquid aside, separately, to cool to room temperature. Peel, devein, and wash the shrimp under cold water. Then bring 1 quart water to a boil in a small pan, drop in the shrimp and cook briskly, uncovered, for about 3 minutes, or until they turn pink and are firm to the touch. Drain and coarsely chop the shrimp. Set aside to cool.

(continued)

Polish Cold Soup with Shrimp   *(continued)*

When the beet cooking liquid is completely cooled, beat in sour cream with a wire whisk. Stir in the beets, shrimp, cucumbers, scallions, radishes, 2 tablespoons of the dill, lemon juice, the remaining vinegar, salt, sugar, and white pepper. Taste for seasoning, cover the bowl tightly with plastic wrap, and refrigerate for at least 3 hours, or until the soup is thoroughly chilled. To serve, ladle the soup into a large chilled tureen or individual soup plates. Sprinkle the remaining dill on top and, if you like, garnish the soup with thin slices of lemon and chopped hard-cooked eggs. Serves 8.

Blueberry Soup

3 tablespoons sugar
1/2 cup water

2 pints blueberries
1 cup sour cream
1/2 cup white wine

Bring sugar and water to a boil and add blueberries. Cook until the blueberries pop. Press this mixture through a sieve and cool. Add sour cream and wine. Serve cold. Serves 4.

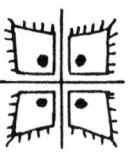

Sorrel Soup

1 tablespoon butter or margarine
2 handfuls of fresh sorrel,
  cleaned and chopped

1 quart chicken broth
1 teaspoon flour
1/2 cup sour cream
2 hard-cooked eggs, quartered

Melt butter in a large pan, add sorrel. Cover and simmer for 5 minutes. Add chicken broth. Bring to a boil. Mix flour with sour cream until smooth. Add to soup. Serve hot; garnish each serving with a quarter of a hard-cooked egg. Serves 8.

Note: If you can't find sorrel, substitute 2 handfuls of fresh, chopped spinach plus 1 tablespoon lemon juice.

Barley Soup

1/2 cup barley
1 1/2 quarts beef stock, recipe
   found on page 32

1 large white potato, diced
2 tablespoons chopped parsley

Clean barley and soak in water for 3 hours. Drain barley. Boil beef stock for 15 minutes. Add barley and cook for 30 minutes. Add potato and cook for 10 more minutes. Serve hot, garnished with parsley. Serves 6.

Decorative wooden plate from Poland.

Rye Flour Kvas

2 cups rye flour   3 to 4 cups lukewarm water

Put flour into a 1 1/2-quart crock and gradually add water, stirring it into the flour until smooth. Cover the crock with a cloth and store in a warm place for 48 hours. The mixture will bubble. The *kvas* is done when brown liquid appears on the top. When you are ready to use it, skim off the foam. Add cold water to fill the crock, stirring it in. Allow the flour to settle for a few hours. Separate the clear liquid and refrigerate the clear liquid in jars. Makes 3 cups.

White Borscht

2 cups water
1 pound white Polish sausage
1 yellow onion, chopped
1 bay leaf
4 peppercorns

2 cups rye flour *kvas*, recipe
found on page 41
1 1/2 teaspoons marjoram
2 cloves garlic, minced
1/2 cup sour cream
salt and pepper

Combine 2 cups water with sausage, onion, bay leaf, and peppercorns. Boil for 30 minutes. Remove sausage, slice it, and return to soup. Stir in rye flour *kvas* and bring to a boil. Add garlic and marjoram. Cook over very low heat for 10 minutes. Carefully stir in sour cream, salt and pepper. Serves 4.

Vegetable Soup

1 1/2 quarts water or meat stock
1/2 onion, sliced
1 leek, sliced
1 carrot, sliced
1 small cauliflower, cut into flowerets
1 parsley root, sliced
1 stalk celery, sliced

1 potato, cubed
6 ounces string beans,
   cut into 1-inch pieces
6 ounces green peas
2 tomatoes, peeled and quartered
1 tablespoon butter
1 teaspoon flour
1 tablespoon chopped dill weed or parsley

Combine meat stock with onion, leek, carrot, cauliflower, parsley root, and celery. Cook 15 minutes over low heat. Add potato, string beans, peas, and tomatoes. Simmer for another 10 minutes. In another pan, melt butter and sprinkle in flour; stir until smooth. Add butter mixture to soup. Bring to a boil. Garnish with chopped dill. Serves 6.

Pea Soup

1 pound smoked bacon
1 1/2 quarts water
1 pound dried yellow peas
1 bay leaf
1 onion, chopped
1 carrot, sliced
1 parsley root, sliced

1 celery root, sliced
1/2 leek, sliced
2 cloves garlic, mashed
2 teaspoons marjoram
1 bouillon cube
1 tablespoon butter
salt and pepper
croutons

Combine bacon with water and boil for 1 hour. Remove meat from broth, dice, and return to soup. Add peas, bay leaf, and vegetables. Cook for 1 hour. Place soup in a blender. Add garlic, marjoram, bouillon cube, and butter and process to purée. Return to pot and cook an additional 15 minutes. Add salt and pepper to taste. Serve with croutons. Serves 6.

Rhubarb and Strawberry Soup

1 pound strawberries, cleaned
1 stalk pink rhubarb, cut into
   1-inch slices

1 quart water
1 tablespoon lemon juice
3 tablespoons sugar
1 cup sour cream

Combine strawberries, rhubarb and water and boil for 5 minutes. Set aside for 1 to 2 hours. Place the soup in a blender, add lemon juice, sugar, and sour cream. Blend until smooth. Serve hot or cold. Serves 6.

Dill Pickle Soup

5 dill pickles, shredded
4 teaspoons butter, divided
1 quart water
1 carrot, chopped
2 celery stalks, chopped

1 parsley root, chopped
1 leek, chopped
1 potato, peeled and cubed
1/2 cup sour cream
2 tablespoons chopped dill

Over very low heat to avoid browning, sauté pickles in 1 teaspoon butter for 20 minutes. In another pot combine water, carrot, celery, parsley, leek, and remaining butter; cook for 20 minutes. Add potato and continue cooking for another 15 minutes. Stir in dill pickle mixture. Bring to a boil, reduce heat, and carefully add sour cream. Garnish with fresh chopped dill. Serves 4.

Mushroom Soup

1 1/2 ounces dried mushrooms
2 yellow onions, sliced
1 pound beef with bone
1 3/4 quarts water
salt and pepper to taste

1 carrot
2 parsley roots
1 celery stalk
2 tablespoons sour cream
1 tablespoon parsley, chopped

Clean mushrooms. Soak in water for 1 to 2 hours. Cook with sliced onions, covered, until tender. Strain and reserve broth; separate mushrooms, and slice. In a separate pot, combine cleaned meat and bones, water, salt, and pepper. Cook slowly for 30 minutes. Add vegetables and cook for another 30 minutes. Set aside to cool for 1 hour. Strain the broth and add it to the mushroom broth. Add mushrooms. Add sour cream and garnish with chopped parsley. Serve hot. Serves 6.
Note: To make this without meat as a Christmas Eve soup, use 1/4 pound butter instead of meat.

White Easter Soup

M. Nancy Stubeusz, Oneonta, New York

3 quarts water
2 cups diced smoked kielbasa
1 onion, chopped
2 cloves garlic, minced
several peppercorns

1 bay leaf
1 cup cream, at room temperature, divided
2 to 3 tablespoons flour
2 to 3 tablespoons vinegar, to taste
2 hard-cooked eggs, sliced or in wedges

Bring water, kielbasa, onion, garlic, peppercorns, and bay leaf to a boil; cover and simmer for 1 hour. Combine about 1 tablespoon of cream with flour, then add this mixture to remaining cream. Stir into soup. Cook over very low heat until slightly thickened. Add vinegar to taste. Serve garnished with hard-cooked eggs. Serves 8.

Borscht

Miriam Canter, Iowa City, Iowa

1 pound of small beets with green tops or 2 1-pound cans of sliced beets, undrained

2 quarts beef stock or bouillon
2 tablespoons lemon juice or vinegar
2 tablespoons sugar

Cut greens from beets, rinse thoroughly, and chop. Scrub beets, peel and slice. In a large saucepan combine sliced beets, chopped greens, stock, and lemon juice or vinegar and sugar. Cover, bring to a boil, and then simmer 30 minutes or until beets are tender. Or cook canned beets 10 to 15 minutes, until beets are tender. Remove from heat, cool, and then chill. Serves 6.

Duck Blood Soup

1/2 duck, cut up (2 to 3 pounds)
1 quart water
1 stalk celery
1 carrot
2 sprigs parsley
3 whole allspice
2 whole cloves

1/2 pound dried pitted prunes
1/2 cup raisins
1/4 cup dried apples or pears
2 tablespoons flour
1 cup sour cream
1 quart duck or goose blood
salt, pepper, and lemon juice to taste

Cover duck with water in a large kettle. Add salt. Bring to a boil. Skim off foam. Put vegetables and spices into a cheesecloth bag and add to the soup. Cover and continue boiling for an hour.

(continued)

Duck Blood Soup   *(continued)*

Remove the spice bag. Remove meat from kettle, remove bones, chop meat, and return it to the soup. Add dried fruit and cook for another 30 minutes. Blend sour cream and flour until smooth. Add blood a little at a time while beating. Add about 1 cup of the hot soup to the sour cream mixture and blend. Pour the mixture into the soup, stirring constantly. Bring the soup to a boil, stirring constantly. Add salt, pepper, and lemon juice to taste. Serves 8 to 10.

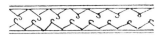

Salads

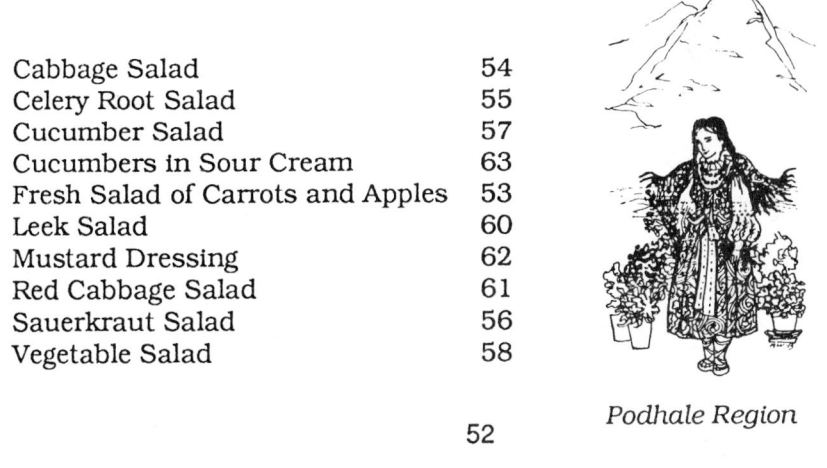

Podhale Region

Fresh Salad of Carrots and Apples

5 large carrots

2 large apples

juice of 1/2 lemon

sugar to taste

Grate the carrots as finely as possible. Grate the apples and add to the carrots. Toss with lemon juice and add sugar to taste. Serve as a salad or as an accompaniment to another dish. Very nutritious. Serves 6 to 8.

Cabbage Salad

3 cups white sweet or savoy
   cabbage, shredded
salt

2 tart apples, shredded
1 small carrot, shredded
1 large onion, shredded

Dressing:
juice of 1/2 lemon
3 tablespoons salad oil

1 teaspoon sugar
salt and pepper
1 tablespoon parsley, chopped

Sprinkle cabbage with salt and then set aside for about an hour; drain off the liquid. Add the remaining ingredients. Toss well.

Dressing: Combine juice, oil, sugar, salt, and pepper, and mix well. Stir into cabbage mixture. Prepare 2 hours before serving. Garnish with parsley. Serves 6.

Celery Root Salad

1 large celery root
salt and pepper to taste
1 tablespoon sour cream

2 tablespoons mayonnaise
1 ounce walnuts, chopped

Grate the celery root and sprinkle with pepper. Set aside for ten minutes. Combine sour cream and mayonnaise; add salt and pepper to taste. Pour sour cream mixture over celery and mix thoroughly. Add nuts and serve. Serves 4.
Note: Celery root is available in most food stores. It is in season in September and early October.

Sauerkraut Salad

1/4 cup salad or olive oil
1 tablespoon sugar
1 teaspoon caraway seed, optional
1/2 teaspoon salt

1/2 teaspoon pepper
1 pound sauerkraut, rinsed,
   drained and chopped
2 tart apples, peeled, cored and diced
3/4 cup grated carrot

Combine oil, sugar and spices. Stir sauerkraut into oil mixture. Add apples and grated carrot. Toss to coat. Very good with fried fish. Serves 4.

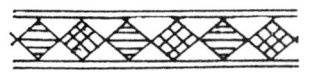

Cucumber Salad

1 cucumber, thinly sliced
salt
2 tablespoons vinegar

1 tablespoon water
pepper
1/2 teaspoon sugar
parsley or chives

Salt cucumber slices and set aside for 1/2 hour. Combine vinegar and water. Add salt, pepper, and sugar. Boil and cool. Strain cucumbers and pour vinegar mixture over cucumbers. Serve garnished with parsley or chives. Serves 3 to 4.

Vegetable Salad

2 medium-sized white potatoes
3 medium-sized carrots
1/2 celery root
1 medium-sized parsley root
3 hard-cooked eggs, diced
2 dill pickles, diced

2 apples, diced
1 4-ounce can green peas
1 leek, diced
1/2 cup sour cream
1/2 cup mayonnaise
1 tablespoon Dijon mustard
salt and pepper to taste

Garnish:
tomatoes

marinated red bell pepper
parsley

(continued)

Vegetable Salad   *(continued)*

Boil potatoes, carrots, celery root, and parsley root in salted water. When tender remove, peel, and finely dice the boiled vegetables. Add eggs, pickles, apples, peas, and leek. Set aside. Combine remaining ingredients. Pour over diced vegetables and mix thoroughly. Garnish with tomato halves, slices of marinated red pepper, and parsley. Serves 6.

Holiday Folk Fair, Milwaukee, Wisconsin

Leek Salad

1 leek, sliced
1 apple, peeled and shredded
juice of 1/2 lemon

2 teaspoons sugar
salt and pepper to taste
mayonnaise

Combine all ingredients and toss to coat with mayonnaise. Refrigerate for 1 to 2 hours.

Red Cabbage Salad

2-pound head red cabbage,
   finely shredded
juice of 1/2 lemon
1 small red onion, finely chopped
2 tart apples, shredded

1 tablespoon sugar
1 teaspoon salt
1 tablespoon olive oil
pepper
1 tablespoon chopped parsley

Boil cabbage for a few minutes; drain. Cabbage becomes violet. Sprinkle with lemon juice and watch the cabbage become red. Add remaining ingredients except parsley, and toss. Refrigerate for 3 hours. Garnish with parsley.

Mustard Dressing

2 tablespoons olive oil
2 hard-cooked egg yolks, mashed
2 shallots, minced
1 teaspoon green onion, chopped
1 teaspoon parsley, chopped

juice of 1/2 lemon
1 teaspoon sugar
2 tablespoons red wine
1/4 cup chicken broth
1/2 cup prepared mustard

Carefully blend olive oil with egg yolks. Add shallots, green onion and parsley, stirring constantly. Stir in lemon juice, sugar, wine, broth, and mustard. Mix well. Serve with cold meat or hard-cooked eggs.

Cucumbers in Sour Cream

Virginia Luty, Hinckley, Ohio

3 cups sliced cucumber
salt to taste

1/4 cup fresh dill or 2 tablespoons
    dry dill weed
1 cup dairy sour cream or yogurt

Sprinkle cucumbers with salt. Let stand for 30 minutes; pat dry with paper towels. Stir dill into sour cream. Add cucumbers and mix well. Serves 4 to 6.

Breads

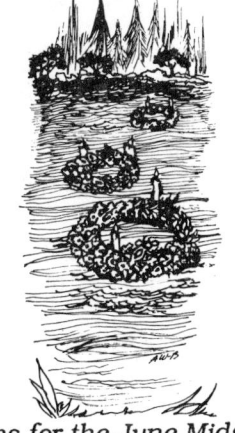

Wreaths for the June Midsummer

Yeast Bread

2 ounces fresh yeast
1/2 cup warm water
2 cups granulated sugar
3/4 cup milk

1 cup margarine or butter
4 eggs
1 teaspoon vanilla extract
1 teaspoon salt
4 cups all-purpose flour

Dissolve yeast in 1/2 cup warm water. Combine sugar, milk, margarine, eggs, vanilla, and salt. Beat well until mixed. Stir in yeast. Let it rise at room temperature overnight, 10 hours. Stir in flour gradually, adding enough flour to make a stiff dough. Set aside for another six hours. Form the dough to fit a greased bread pan and let rise for another 1 to 2 hours. Bake at 350° for about 45 minutes or until golden.

Pumpkin Muffins

Lorraine Goszewski, Heritage Inn, West Seneca, New York

1 cup sifted all-purpose flour
1/2 cup sugar
2 teaspoons baking powder
1/2 teaspoon cinnamon
1/2 teaspoon nutmeg
1/4 teaspoon salt

1/4 cup butter or margarine
1 egg
1/2 cup evaporated milk
1/2 cup canned pumpkin
1/2 cup seedless raisins
1 tablespoon sugar, for topping

Sift dry ingredients together and cut in butter. Combine egg, evaporated milk, and pumpkin. Stir in raisins. Add egg mixture to dry ingredients, stirring just enough to mix. Fill greased muffin tins 2/3 full. Sprinkle sugar over the tops. Bake at 400° for 20 to 25 minutes.

Graham Bread

6 to 7 cups whole-wheat flour
2 1/2 cups graham flour
1 cake yeast

1 tablespoon sugar
2 1/2 cups warm milk, divided
1 tsp. salt

In a large bowl sift flours together and set aside. Dissolve yeast and sugar in 1/2 cup warm milk; set aside 10 minutes. Make a well in the flour and pour the yeast mixture into the hole. Stir yeast mixture into the flour, adding salt and enough of the remaining milk to make a soft dough. Place in a greased bowl, cover and let rise until doubled. Punch down and knead until smooth and elastic. Divide dough in half and shape into loaves. Place each of the loaves into greased and floured loaf pans. Cover and let rise until doubled. Bake at 450° for 1 hour or until the loaves test done. Brush with water while bread is hot. Great for breakfast.

Note: You may shape this dough into rolls or small cakes.

Buckwheat Bread

Rosemary A. Kirchner, Polish Museum, Winona, Minnesota

1 3/4 cups buttermilk
1/2 cup brown sugar
2 cups buckwheat flour

1 1/2 teaspoons salt
1/2 teaspoon baking powder
1/2 cup coarsely chopped prunes,
   or raisins

Grease an 8 1/2x4 1/2-inch loaf pan and line it with greased waxed paper. Combine all ingredients in order given and pour into prepared pan. Work the batter into the corners of the pan with a spatula and level off the top. Set aside for 10 minutes while oven heats to 350°, 300° if a glass pan is used. Bake loaf for 45 minutes or until loaf tests done. Place loaf on side and gently remove the waxed paper to slip loaf onto a rack to cool.

Dark Rye Bread

Frances A. Mleczko is a second generation Polish-American who founded the Marian Nursing Home in her hometown, Radisson, Wisconsin. Her parents came from Poland to Chicago in 1913. They bought brush land in Wisconsin, and raised seven children. Once there were many Polish farmers in the area, but farming was not very good. Her aged mother lives in the nursing home.

2 cups milk, scalded
2 tablespoons butter
2 tablespoons sugar
1 teaspoon salt

1 package active dry yeast
1/2 cup lukewarm water
4 cups rye flour, divided
2 1/2 cups whole-wheat flour
2 tablespoons caraway seed

(continued)

Dark Rye Bread   *(continued)*

Pour scalded milk over butter, sugar and salt in a large bowl; stir. Cool. Dissolve yeast in lukewarm water. Add softened yeast and 3 cups rye flour to milk mixture. Beat thoroughly, then beat in remaining rye flour. Cover and let rise in a warm place until doubled in bulk. Turn onto well-floured board. Knead in whole-wheat flour and caraway seed. Knead until dough is smooth. Divide in half and shape into 2 rounds or into oblong loaves in greased loaf pans. Cover and let rise in warm place until doubled in bulk. Bake at 450° for 15 minutes; reduce heat to 350° and bake 35 to 40 minutes longer. Brush with melted butter 5 minutes before done if a more tender crust is desired.

Main Dishes

Stuffed Cabbage

2 dried rolls, or Italian bread
1 pound ground beef
1 pound ground pork
1 large yellow onion, chopped
1 egg

salt and pepper to taste
1 head cabbage, preferably with
   large leaves
1/2 pound bacon
1 tablespoon flour

Soak the rolls in water for 15 to 20 minutes. Remove and squeeze dry. Combine meats, rolls, and onion. Add egg, salt, and pepper. Mix well and set aside. Cut out the core of the cabbage. Place cabbage in boiling water for 3 minutes.

(continued)

Stuffed Cabbage   *(continued)*

Remove cabbage from water and drain. Separate leaves from head if possible and scald again to soften if necessary. Repeat process until all leaves are separated. Cut off the thick parts of the cabbage leaves to make folding easier. Take a small leaf of cabbage and place a large spoonful of stuffing on it. Fold a large leaf around it like an envelope. Secure with a toothpick. Continue until you have used all the leaves and stuffing. Fry the bacon to get the fat. Remove bacon from pan and drain the grease into a dish. Heat 3 tablespoons of the fat into a Dutch oven or wide, deep pot. Put approximately 10 stuffed cabbage leaves into the pot and simmer for 1/2 hour, adding water as needed. Cook all stuffed cabbage leaves this way. To prepare a sauce for the stuffed cabbage leaves, use 2 tablespoons of the bacon fat and the flour; stir until smooth. Add water from the cooked cabbage rolls to make a sauce of the correct consistency. Pour over cabbage leaves and simmer for about 15 minutes.

Beef Slices

2 pounds beef, eye of round, top
   round or sirloin; cut in 6 thin steaks
salt and pepper
1/2 cup all-purpose flour

1 teaspoon salt
1/2 teaspoon pepper
3 tablespoons butter or other fat
1/2 cup water
1/2 cup sour cream

Filling:
1 pickle, cut lengthwise into 6 wedges

1 onion, sliced
5 slices bacon, cut into small pieces

(continued)

Beef Slices   *(continued)*

Pound meat. Sprinkle with salt and pepper. Let it stand for 30 minutes. Pound again until thin. Roll a piece of pickle, onion and bacon into each slice of beef. Secure with a toothpick. Combine flour, salt and pepper. Coat each roll with the flour mixture. Brown each roll on all sides in the butter over high heat. Add 1/2 cup water and simmer about 60 minutes. Blend 3 tablespoons of the juices from the pan with the sour cream until smooth. Add sour cream mixture to the meat. Bring to a boil and simmer for 5 minutes. Serve with noodles or boiled buckwheat.

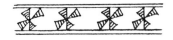

Mixed Meats in a Fresh Pepper Sauce

1 pound of each meat: beef, veal, and pork, cut into 1-inch cubes
2 tablespoons flour
2 tablespoons vegetable oil
3 onions, cut in quarters
2 green peppers, cut in squares, divided
2 cups beef broth
salt and pepper to taste
1 teaspoon dried red pepper
1 bay leaf
1 clove garlic
3 tomatoes, cut in quarters
1 teaspoon caraway seeds, optional
1/2 cup dairy sour cream, optional

Coat meats with flour, then brown in oil. Set aside. In the same skillet brown onions. Combine meat and onions; add 1/2 the green peppers, broth, salt, pepper, red pepper, bay leaf, and garlic. Simmer 45 minutes. Add the remaining green peppers and cook for another 15 minutes. Add tomatoes 5 minutes before serving. Blend caraway seeds and sour cream into sauce, if desired. Serve with noodles. Serves 6 to 8.

Warsaw-Style Tripe

2 pounds fresh tripe
1 pound veal bones
salt and pepper
2 carrots, sliced
3 stalks celery, sliced
1 onion, chopped
1 tablespoon fresh parsley, chopped

2 teaspoons marjoram
1/4 teaspoon ginger
1/4 teaspoon mace
2 cups meat broth
2 tablespoons butter or margarine
1 tablespoon flour
1/2 cup light cream

Rinse tripe thoroughly under running cold water. In a large kettle, combine tripe and veal bones with enough water to cover. Add salt. Bring to a boil, reduce heat, and cook 4 to 5 hours, or until the tripe is tender.

(continued)

Warsaw-Style Tripe *(continued)*

Drain the tripe; discard the bones and cooking liquid. Cut tripe into very thin strips. Cook the strips with vegetables and spices in meat broth until the vegetables are tender. Melt butter in a pan and stir in flour until smooth and golden. Blend in a small amount of the broth from the tripe mixture. Add salt and pepper. Add cream gradually. Drain vegetables and tripe. Stir into sauce. Simmer another 5 minutes.

Chicken Scaloppine in Vegetable Sauce

Orbit Restaurant, Chicago, Illinois

4 boneless chicken breasts
3 tablespoons flour
3 tablespoons grated
    Parmesan cheese

2 eggs, beaten
1/2 cup bread crumbs
3 tablespoons margarine

Sauce:

2 carrots
1 parsley root
2 stalks celery
2 tomatoes, peeled
3 green onions, chopped

2 tablespoons water or broth
1 tablespoon potato starch
1/2 cup apple juice
1/2 teaspoon oregano
juice from 1/2 lemon
salt and pepper

(continued)

Chicken Scaloppine in Vegetable Sauce   *(continued)*

Sauce: Clean and chop all vegetables and place in a large pot; add water or broth and simmer until very tender. Blend potato starch with apple juice until smooth. Add to vegetable mixture, stirring constantly. Add remaining ingredients to taste and set aside.

Chicken: Pound chicken breasts until thin. Combine flour and Parmesan cheese. Coat each piece of chicken with flour mixture; dip each into the beaten eggs and then the bread crumbs. Quickly brown the chicken in margarine on both sides. Pour sauce over chicken; simmer until chicken is tender. Serve with mashed potatoes or rice.

Marinated Steak

Marinade:

4 cups red cooking wine
3/4 cup oil

1 bay leaf
1 large onion, halved

Steak:

2 pounds beef, cut into thick slices

3 tablespoons oil
salt and pepper to taste

Combine marinade ingredients. Marinate beef overnight. Remove from marinade and pat dry with paper towels, reserving marinade. Brown meat in oil on both sides. Pour marinade over browned meat and season to taste. Simmer over low heat until meat is tender. Serve with potatoes. Serves 4 to 5.

Stuffed Cutlet with Mushrooms

Orbit Restaurant, Chicago, Illinois

2 pounds pork roast, cut into
   1-inch thick cutlets
3 tablespoons flour
2 eggs, beaten

3 tablespoons bread crumbs
salt and pepper
3 tablespoons margarine or oil, divided
1/2 cup water

Stuffing:
1/2 pound mushrooms, sliced
1 onion, chopped

1 tablespoon margarine
2 hard-cooked eggs, sliced
salt and pepper

82

(continued)

Stuffed Cutlet with Mushrooms   *(continued)*

Stuffing: Sauté mushrooms and onion in margarine until soft. Add hard-cooked eggs, salt and pepper, and cook for 3 minutes. Set aside.

Cutlets: Beat cutlets until thin. Place a heaping tablespoon of stuffing on each cutlet; roll it around filling. Secure with toothpicks or tie with twine. Coat meat rolls with the flour; dip first in beaten eggs and then in bread crumbs seasoned with salt and pepper. Brown the meat in the margarine on all sides. Add half a cup of water, cover and simmer for 5 minutes. Serve with mashed potatoes.

Chicken Fricassee

Adela Zydel, Worcester, New York, writes: "This recipe was served at my aunt's summer resort. The guests clamored for seconds."

1 chicken
2 cups chicken broth
2 tablespoons butter
2 tablespoons flour
1/2 cup heavy cream

1/2 cup milk
1 tablespoon chopped fresh parsley
1/4 teaspoon dill
salt and pepper to taste
1 small can peas
cooked rice

Cut chicken into serving-sized pieces. Cook chicken in broth until tender; add butter. Dissolve flour in the cream and add to the chicken. Add milk, parsley, dill, salt, and pepper. Over low heat cook another 10 minutes, stirring constantly. Add peas, cook 1 minute. Remove from heat and let stand for 5 minutes. Serve over cooked rice. Can be refrigerated or frozen and used at a later date.

Polish Hunter's Stew

Lucyna Migala, Chicago, Illinois

2 pounds sauerkraut
1/2 pound pork, cut into small pieces
1/2 pound veal, cut into small pieces
1/2 pound venison, rabbit or other
   wild game cut into small pieces
1/2 pound Polish sausage, cut into
   small pieces
1/2 pound bacon, cut into strips
any other leftover meat, optional
1 small cabbage, sliced, optional
2 dried mushrooms

3 medium-sized onions, coarsely
   chopped
butter
1 pound fresh mushrooms, sliced
3 small ripe tomatoes, peeled and sliced
2 bay leaves, optional
2 large apples, peeled, cored and
   sliced, optional
1 tablespoon caraway seed
1/2 cup red or white wine
salt and pepper to taste
sugar to taste

(continued)

Polish Hunter's Stew   *(continued)*

Put sauerkraut with its juice in a large pot; if a less strong taste is desired, drain the sauerkraut and replace the juice with fresh boiled water. Bring to a boil on medium heat; reduce heat and simmer. Fry bacon. Brown pork, veal, venison, rabbit, or other fresh meat and Polish sausage in bacon grease. Cook until almost done, then add to kraut. Add any leftover ham or other smoked meat or any other cooked meat, all cut into small cubes. Add cabbage. Soak dry mushrooms in 1/2 cup water until soft; dice and add to kraut with the water they were soaked in. Brown the onions in butter; add fresh mushrooms and sauté until just about done. Add entire contents of skillet to kraut pot. Add tomatoes for color. Add bay leaves and apples for sweetening; this will cause a less "wild" taste, if desired. Add caraway seed. Simmer for 3 to 4 hours, stirring often until all ingredients blend into a golden brown color. It is best to make this a day or two ahead and let it simmer an hour or two each day, adding ingredients each day if desired. Just before serving add wine, salt, pepper, and sugar; stir. Polish hunter's stew is traditionally served with hard-crust rye bread or parboiled potatoes.

Sausage in Beer

Slotkowski Sausage Company, Chicago, Illinois

1 pound Slotkowski Smoked
   Polish sausage
4 potatoes, with skins, cut in 8ths

2 green peppers, cut in strips
1 onion, thinly sliced
3/4 to 1 can beer
pepper to taste

Place all ingredients in casserole dish. Cover with foil, bake at 325° for 30 to 45 minutes, turning vegetables occasionally until potatoes are done. Remove foil for the last 15 minutes of baking. Serve with black bread.

Marinated Herring

This dish is very popular for Shrovetide.

2 salted herring	2 white peppercorns
1 cup water	3 black peppercorns
1 onion, thinly sliced	1 cup vinegar
2 bay leaves	2 teaspoons sugar

Soak the herring in cold water for 24 hours, changing water after the first 6 hours. Clean herring, remove skin and bones, cut lengthwise. Place herring in a jar. Boil water, onion, spices, and vinegar together. Cool and add sugar. Pour the mixture over the herring. Cover the jar and refrigerate for 24 to 48 hours.

Stuffed Baked Fish

This has been very popular in Poland.

1 dressed pike or carp, 4 to 5 pounds
salt and pepper
1/3 cup butter or margarine
2 onions, chopped
2 stalks celery, chopped
1/2 cup chopped parsley
1 cup dried chopped apple

1 cup mushrooms, chopped
1 cup water or white wine
3 cups dry bread cubes
2 teaspoons sugar
2 teaspoons lemon juice
3 eggs, beaten
butter, melted

Sprinkle fish with salt and pepper. Set aside for 2 hours. Sauté onion in butter until golden; add celery, parsley, apple, and mushrooms; fry for 2 more minutes.

89

(continued)

Stuffed Baked Fish   *(continued)*

Add water or wine, bread cubes, sugar, lemon juice, and eggs . Mix well. Fill fish cavity with the stuffing. Close and secure with skewers or toothpicks. Place fish in a roasting pan and drizzle with melted butter. Bake at 350° for about 40 minutes, or until the fish flakes easily.

Carp in Aspic

This dish is served on Christmas Eve.

1 medium-sized carp, well-gutted
    and scaled, with cut and
    separated head, also well-gutted
1 carrot
2 sprigs parsley
1/4 a medium-sized celery root

1 leek, sliced
1 yellow onion, sliced
1 bay leaf
8 peppercorns
1 white peppercorn
1 envelope unflavored gelatin, if needed

Boil all the vegetables and spices for 10 minutes in water to cover. Cut the prepared carp into 1-inch slices. Add the pieces and the carp head to the vegetables and boil for 20 minutes. Remove the fish and vegetables with a slotted spoon. Debone the fish and place in a mold or bowl; garnish with vegetables. Check broth; if it is not stiff soften gelatin in 1/4 cup cold water, then dissolve in 1 cup hot water. Pour over fish. Refrigerate until set. Serve cold.

Carp

This is a dish served for Christmas Eve supper.

1 medium-sized carp, scaled and
    well-gutted
salt and pepper to taste

1 cup flour
1 cup bread crumbs
2 eggs, beaten
2 tablespoons vegetable oil

Cut fish into 1-inch slices; salt and pepper slices. Place the flour into a dish, the bread crumbs into another and eggs into a third dish. Heat the oil in a frying pan. Dip fish slices in the flour, then in the eggs, and then in the bread crumbs. Fry until golden. Serve hot, straight from the pan.

Herring in Sour Cream with Onion and Apple

1 salted herring
1 tablespoon vegetable oil
1/2 cup vinegar
1 yellow onion, thinly sliced

1 apple, peeled and sliced
1/2 cup sour cream
1/2 teaspoon sugar
1 tablespoon mayonnaise
2 tablespoons chopped parsley

Clean herring and soak in cold water for 24 hours, changing water after the first 6 hours. Clean herring again; remove skin. Fillet herring, removing bones; cut into 1-inch cubes. Sprinkle with oil and vinegar; set aside for 2 hours. Meanwhile, scald the onion. Cool. Combine the onion and apple. Cover each piece of herring with the onion-apple mixture. Combine the sour cream, sugar, and mayonnaise; pour over herring. Garnish with parsley.

Polish Hot Pot

Kowalski Sausage Company, Hamtramck, Michigan

6 large potatoes
1/2 pound Polish sausage or bologna
6 onions, sliced thick

1 1-pound can tomatoes
1 1/2 teaspoons paprika
1 teaspoon salt
1/2 cup sour cream

Pare potatoes and cut into 1/2-inch slices. Arrange in bottom of large greased casserole. Cut sausage into 1- or 2-inch cubes and place over potatoes. Top with thick onion slices. Combine tomatoes, paprika and salt; add to casserole. Bake at 350° for 45 minutes. Stir in sour cream and bake 15 minutes longer. Makes 6 servings.

Kielbasa and Cabbage

Kowalski Sausage Company, Hamtramck, Michigan
A crock pot special. A regal feast made with popular dinner sausage.

1 small head cabbage, coarsely diced
3 small potatoes, peeled and diced
1 teaspoon salt
1/2 teaspoon caraway seed

1 onion, sliced
1 1/2 pounds kielbasa sausage,
   cut into 1-inch pieces
1 14-ounce can chicken broth

Put vegetables, seasonings, and sausage in a crock pot. Pour in chicken broth. Cover. Cook on low 6 to 10 hours, or on high 2 to 4 hours. Serves 4.

Grandma K's Fresh Kielbasa with Sauerkraut

Ronald J. Kowalski, Kowalski Sausage Company, Hamtramck, Michigan

1 pound fresh kielbasa links	1 bay leaf
6 tablespoons water	1/2 teaspoon garlic salt
3 large onions, chopped	1 cup chicken broth
1 large apple, diced	8 cups sauerkraut, well drained
1/4 cup chopped parsley	1/2 cup white wine
	2 tablespoons brown sugar

Pierce kielbasa links in several places. In a 3-quart casserole, over medium heat, brown sausages well with water; remove and cool. Drain all but 2 tablespoons of fat. Add onion, apple, parsley, bay leaf, garlic salt, and chicken broth; simmer covered for 20 minutes. Stir in sauerkraut, wine, sugar, and sausage links sliced into 1/4-inch pieces. Bake, covered, 1 hour at 350°. Serve with boiled or mashed potatoes for a hearty satisfying meal. Serves 8.

Pierogi

2 cups flour

2 eggs
few teaspoons water

Combine all ingredients to make a firm dough. Divide dough and roll into thin sheets on a floured board. Cut into circles about 3 1/2 inches in diameter. Place a spoonful of your favorite filling on half the circle. Fold over and press edges together. If dough won't seal, put some water on the edges and pinch together. Place *pierogi* into boiling salted water. Cook 5 minutes. Remove from water with slotted spoon and serve with melted butter. Or cook *pierogi* in butter until lightly browned. Makes about 35.

Pierogi Fillings

Mushroom Filling:

1/2 pound mushrooms, finely diced	3 tablespoons sour cream
2 tablespoons butter	1 teaspoon dill
	salt and pepper to taste

Sauté mushrooms in butter. Remove from heat; cool. Add remaining ingredients. Use to fill *pierogi* dough as directed.

Sausage Filling:

1/2 pound Polish sausage, chopped	1/4 cup beer
1/4 cup finely diced onion	1/2 cup bread crumbs
	salt and pepper to taste

Cook Polish sausage and onion together until the meat is no longer pink. Add remaining ingredients and use to fill *pierogi* dough as directed.

(continued)

Pierogi Fillings   *(continued)*

Cheese Filling:

1 cup grated farmers' cheese or   salt and pepper
  dry cottage cheese   finely chopped green onions to taste

Combine all ingredients and use to fill *pierogi*.

Sauerkraut Filling:

1 small can sauerkraut   1 teaspoon butter
1 small onion, chopped fine   salt and pepper

Cook a small can of sauerkraut for about 20 minutes. Rinse in cold water and squeeze dry. Sauté onion in butter and add to sauerkraut. Add salt and pepper and fill *pierogi*.

(continued)

Pierogi Fillings   *(continued)*

Potato Filling:

butter	2 cups mashed potatoes, hot
1 medium-sized onion, finely chopped	salt and pepper
	1/2 cup grated sharp Cheddar cheese

Sauté onion in butter until golden. Combine all ingredients and shape into potato balls, place on dough and complete as directed on page 102.

Plum Filling:
1 large can pitted plums

Wrap plums in dough.

    (continued)

Pierogi Fillings *(continued)*

Cheese and Potato Filling:

1 1/2 cups dry cottage cheese
1 1/2 cups mashed potatoes,
   made with butter alone

2 to 4 large onions, minced
salt and pepper to taste

Combine all ingredients and mix well. Let cool and fill *pierogi* with desired amount.
Fills about 70 *pierogi*.

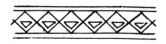

Easy Pierogi Dough

Virginia Luty, Hinckley, Ohio

3 ounces cream cheese

2 cups flour
1/2 cup warm water

Cut the cream cheese into flour. Add water and knead very little. Divide dough and roll into thin sheets on a floured board. Cut into circles about 3 1/2 inches in diameter. Place a spoonful of your favorite filling on half the circle. Fold over and press edges together. If dough won't seal, put some water on the edges and pinch together. Place *pierogi* into boiling salted water. Cook 5 minutes. Remove from water with slotted spoon and serve with melted butter. Or cook *pierogi* in butter until lightly browned. Makes about 35.

Herring in Oil

4 salted herring
1/4 cup wine vinegar, divided

2 onions, chopped
1/2 cup olive oil
1/2 cup chopped green onions

Soak herring in water for 24 hours, changing water after the first 6 hours. Drain herring. Remove skin and bones. Cut into 1-inch slices. Place slices on a serving dish. Sprinkle them with half the vinegar on both sides. Arrange chopped onion around fish. Pour oil and remaining vinegar over fish. Garnish with green onions. Prepare at least 1 hour before serving.

Stuffed Peppers

6 red bell peppers, cored
2 tablespoons butter, divided
2 onions, chopped
1 carrot, sliced
1 parsley root, sliced
1 leek, sliced

2 stalks celery, sliced
1 bay leaf
1/2 cup chicken broth
salt and pepper
1 teaspoon flour
3 tablespoons sour cream

Filling:
12 ounces ground pork
12 ounces ground beef
2 kaiser rolls, soaked in water

1 large onion, shredded
1 egg
salt and pepper

(continued)

Stuffed Peppers   *(continued)*

Filling: Combine all ingredients and mix well.

Stuff each pepper with filling and place them into a greased casserole. Set aside. Sauté onions in 1 teaspoon of butter until golden. In a different frying pan sauté all the vegetables and bay leaf in remaining butter over low heat for 15 minutes. Cover prepared peppers with onion and vegetables. Add broth, cover casserole, and simmer for 10 minutes. Blend flour with sour cream and place 1 teaspoon of this on each pepper. Keep covered and simmer for another 10 minutes.

Kidney Stew

1 pound kidneys
2 tablespoons butter or vegetable oil
3 large onions, chopped
1 bay leaf

1/2 cup chicken broth
salt and pepper
2 teaspoons flour
1/2 cup water
1 teaspoon marjoram

Soak kidneys in cold water for 2 hours, changing water after 30 minutes. Boil enough water to cover kidneys, add the kidneys, and bring to a boil. Drain well. Repeat the boiling twice. Rinse kidneys under warm water and slice thin. Melt butter and add kidneys, onions, bay leaf, broth, salt, and pepper. Bring to a boil. Reduce heat and simmer for 2 hours. Stir together water and flour; add this mixture and the marjoram to the kidney mixture. Serve with boiled buckwheat.

Chicken in Aspic

1 big chicken, cleaned
1 carrot
1 stalk celery
2 parsley roots
1 leek
1 onion

1 bay leaf
salt and pepper to taste
1 ounce unflavored gelatin
2 hard-cooked eggs, optional
1/2 cup green peas
chopped parsley and lemon juice

Place chicken in a big pot, cover with water and bring to a boil. Skim off foam. Add the vegetables except peas. Add bay leaf and salt. Cook until chicken is tender. Set aside to cool. Discard skin and bones; dice meat. Slice the carrot. Discard remaining vegetables and bay leaf. Strain off bouillon; skim off fat. Dissolve gelatin in a little water. Stir into bouillon; bring to a boil. In 4 serving dishes arrange halved eggs face down with carrots and peas. Put meat into each serving dish, and cover with bouillon. Refrigerate until stiff. Garnish with chopped parsley and sprinkle with lemon juice.

Polish Sausage

1/2 pound veal
1/2 pound beef
1 pound pork, diced
1/2 pound pork fat, diced
15 white peppercorns, crushed

15 black peppercorns, crushed
2 tablespoons salt
4 cloves garlic, mashed
1 teaspoon saltpeter
1/2 pint water
3 yards sausage casing

Grind beef and veal in a meat grinder. Combine ground mixture with pork and pork fat. Add peppercorns, salt, garlic, saltpeter, and water. Mix for 15 minutes using a large spoon. Clean and dry sausage casing, using salted hands. With a sausage stuffer, stuff casing with meat mixture and tie off 11-inch sausages. Set aside in a cold place for 3 days, turning the sausage each day. Hang sausages for 5 hours in a chimney or meat smoker to smoke. Boil and serve. Makes 9 sausages.

Stuffed Baked Turkey

1 turkey, 6 to 9 pounds
2 ounces lard

3 teaspoons butter
salt and pepper to taste

Liver Stuffing:
4 kaiser rolls
1 cup milk
1/2 pound turkey liver
1/4 cup butter

3 eggs, separated
1/2 cup chopped parsley
1 tablespoon bread crumbs
salt and pepper
pinch nutmeg

(continued)

Stuffed Baked Turkey   *(continued)*

Clean and rinse turkey, removing all entrails. Sprinkle turkey with salt.

Stuffing: Soak rolls in milk. Drain and place in a blender with liver; blend. Cream butter and egg yolks, add liver mixture and parsley; beat well. Beat egg whites until stiff. Carefully blend egg whites into liver mixture. Add remaining ingredients. Melt lard in a turkey roaster. Stuff turkey cavities with stuffing. Close cavities and place back down in a turkey roaster. Place butter on top of turkey and bake at 450° for 2 to 3 hours, basting occasionally.

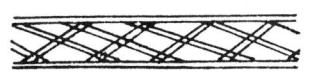

Roast Lamb with Garlic

1 leg of lamb
4 cloves garlic or to taste
1/4 cup vegetable oil

1 tablespoon dried crushed rosemary
salt and pepper to taste

Preheat oven to 450°. With a very sharp knife make 1-inch deep holes all over leg of lamb. Cut each garlic clove into slivers, about 4 to 6 per clove. Insert the garlic slivers into the holes in the lamb. Rub the lamb with oil, rosemary, salt, and pepper. Place lamb in oven and reduce heat to 325°. Bake for 2 1/2 hours.

Vegetables & Side Dishes

Lowicz Region

Wheat with Poppyseeds and Honey

Christmas Eve Dish

1 cup cracked wheat
3/4 cup poppyseed
1/4 cup crushed walnuts

1/4 cup raisins
vanilla extract
sugar and honey
1/2 cup sweet cream

Clean the wheat and boil it in water until tender, about 3 to 4 hours. Drain and cool. Pour poppyseeds in boiling water and continue to boil until the seeds are so tender that they melt in your hand. Drain through a very fine strainer. Put through the grinder, and add to wheat. Add the walnuts, raisins, vanilla, sugar, and honey to taste, and the sweet cream. Mix together and serve in a bowl.

Lenten Compote

2 quarts water
8 ounces dried pitted prunes
5 ounces dried apples
5 ounces dried pears

5 ounces dried apricots
3 dried figs
juice of 1/2 lemon
sugar

Combine the water and the dried fruit. Bring to a boil, reduce heat and simmer over low heat for 10 to 15 minutes. Add lemon juice and sugar to taste. Prepare at least 3 hours before serving. Serve cool.

Sauerkraut

Slotkowski Sausage Company, Chicago, Illinois

2 pounds sauerkraut
6 slices smoked bacon
2 tablespoons bacon fat
1 carrot, sliced
1 large onion, sliced
salt and black pepper

4 juniper berries, crushed, optional
1 tablespoon caraway seed
2 cups white wine
1 1/2 cups chicken stock or water
1 garlic sausage
4 to 6 frankfurters

Put drained sauerkraut into a colander and steep in cold water for 20 minutes, changing water twice.

(continued)

Sauerkraut   *(continued)*

Drain and squeeze dry, then unravel strands of cabbage as much as possible. Preheat oven to 300°. Cut smoked bacon into strips 2 inches long. Melt fat in a flameproof casserole and then fry bacon, carrot, and onion lightly, without browning. Stir in sauerkraut, a generous seasoning of black pepper, and salt. Add juniper berries, if used, caraway seed, wine, and stock or water. Bring to a simmering point; cover tightly and transfer to center of oven. Cook for 3 hours, then add the garlic sausage, pushing it into center of the sauerkraut. Continue cooking another 1 to 1 1/2 hours. Add frankfurters 20 minutes before serving. Check seasoning and serve.

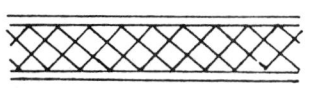

Simmered Mushrooms

1 pound mushrooms
2 teaspoons butter
2 large yellow onions, chopped
small carrot, chopped, optional

1/4 cup chopped parsley, optional
3 tablespoons sour cream
1 teaspoon flour
salt and pepper to taste

Clean and thinly slice the mushrooms. Place into a pot of boiling water for a few seconds and drain. Melt butter in a medium-sized pan and add mushrooms, onions, carrot, and parsley, if used. Add salt and pepper and simmer for one hour, adding water if needed. Combine sour cream and flour. Reduce heat and pour the sour cream mixture over the mushrooms. Simmer for 15 minutes. Season to taste.

Beets Purée

6 medium-sized cooked beets, peeled
3 tablespoons butter
1 tablespoon flour, dissolved
   in 1/4 cup water

2 tablespoons lemon juice
1 teaspoon salt
1 tablespoon sugar
1 tablespoon sour cream

Grate the beets into a pan and, stirring constantly, add all the ingredients except the sour cream. Cover and simmer for about 10 minutes. Stir in sour cream. Serve hot.

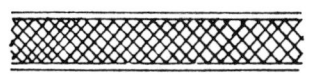

Saucy Dill Mustard

Kowalski Sausage Company, Hamtramck, Michigan
Try this zippy mustard on Kielbasa sausage.

1/2 cup prepared brown mustard
2 tablespoons sugar

1/4 cup salad oil
1/2 cup chopped fresh dill
1/2 cup white wine vinegar

Combine mustard, sugar, and oil. Mix well with wooden spoon. Add dill and vinegar. Beat well. Cover, refrigerate several hours. Makes 1 1/4 cups.

Noodles with Poppyseed and Raisins

2 cups egg noodles, cooked	1 teaspoon vanilla extract
2 tablespoons melted butter	1 teaspoon lemon juice
1/4 cup poppyseeds	1 1/2 teaspoons grated lemon rind
2 tablespoons sugar, or to taste	1/3 cup raisins

Toss cooked noodles with melted butter. Combine poppyseeds with sugar, vanilla extract, lemon juice, lemon rind, and raisins. Add noodles and mix well. Serve warm. Serves 6.

Dill Pickles

1 quart water
2 tablespoons salt
2 pounds pickling cucumbers

10 stalks fresh dill weed
5 cloves garlic
2 inches horseradish root

Boil water with salt. Let cool to lukewarm. Arrange cucumbers in a stoneware jar. Add dill, garlic, and horseradish root. Add the salted water. Cover with an upside-down plate and a weight on the plate. Set aside for 4 to 5 days in the summer or 7 to 8 days in the winter.

Cooked Sauerkraut

1/2 pound pork bones
1 quart water
2 pounds sauerkraut, drained
1 bay leaf
2 white peppercorns

1/2 cube of beef bouillon
salt and pepper to taste
6 ounces bacon, sliced
3 onions, diced
1 tablespoon flour

Boil pork bones in water to make a broth. Remove bones; add sauerkraut and spices. Cook for 1 hour. Fry bacon and onions together. Remove browned bacon and onions to sauerkraut mixture. Sprinkle bacon grease with flour and stir until smooth. Add to sauerkraut. Cook for 15 minutes. Prepare a day ahead.

Potato Pancakes

2 pounds potatoes
1 large onion, minced

1 egg, beaten
3/4 cup flour
salt and pepper to taste

Clean and peel the potatoes. Grate very finely. Add the onion, egg, flour, salt, and pepper. Blend well. If the mixture becomes too runny, add a tablespoon of flour. Fry small pancakes in a hot pan with a little oil. Turn the pancakes to brown on both sides. Very good alone or with a meat sauce. Often served with applesauce or sour cream. Serves 6.

Beets with Horseradish

This dish is typically used for Easter.

2 horseradish roots
salt
3 small beets

boiling water
2 teaspoons sugar
juice of 1 lemon

Soak the horseradish in water for 6 hours. Then peel the roots. Finely grate roots and sprinkle them with salt to prevent darkening. Set aside. Boil the beets for 30 minutes, cool, then peel them. Grate the beets. Scald the horseradish with boiling water; drain. Combine 1 teaspoon salt, sugar, and lemon juice together with 1/2 cup boiling water. Add to the horseradish. Add grated beets and mix well. Put into a jar. Keep in refrigerator. Serve as a side dish.

Cabbage with Mushrooms

1 pound sauerkraut
3 medium-sized yellow onions,
   sliced, divided

1/2 cup butter or vegetable oil, divided
1/2 pound fresh mushrooms
salt and pepper

Drain sauerkraut and chop it fine. Place in a Dutch oven; add water just to cover. Add 2 onions and half the butter. Simmer for 1 1/2 hours, stirring and adding water if needed. Sauté the whole mushrooms in half of the remaining butter and a little water. Salt and pepper to taste. Remove mushrooms and reserve the liquid. Chop mushrooms and add the mushrooms and liquid to sauerkraut. Sauté remaining onion in remaining butter until golden. Add to sauerkraut. Salt and pepper to taste and cook for 20 minutes. Serves 8.

Note: This dish is better if prepared a day in advance and kept in refrigerator.

Desserts

Podhale Region

Nut Roll

Mrs. Helen Pett, Allen Park, Michigan.

Dough:
6 1/2 cups flour, sifted
3 tablespoons sugar
1/2 teaspoon salt
1 cup butter or margarine, softened

3 large eggs, beaten
2 packages dry yeast dissolved in
   1/2 cup warm water
1 cup evaporated milk

Filling:
3 cups ground walnuts
3 sticks oleo or butter

1 1/2 cups sugar
3/4 cup milk
2 egg yolks

(continued)

Nut Roll *(continued)*

Dough: Put flour, sugar, and salt in a large bowl. Add butter, beaten eggs, yeast mixture, and evaporated milk. Blend until well-combined. Knead on a slightly floured board until dough is smooth and elastic. Mixer with a dough hook can be used. If dough is too sticky, add more flour. Put dough aside, cover, and prepare filling.

Filling: Mix ingredients and cook for 5 minutes. Cool.

Assembly: Divide dough into 4 parts. Roll each into a circle about 11 to 12 inches in diameter. Spread with nut filling. Roll up like a jellyroll. Pinch edges together. Place on greased baking sheet and let rise in a warm place until doubled in bulk, about 45 minutes. Preheat oven to 350°. Bake for 25 to 40 minutes. Keep checking until brown.

Note: Other suggested fillings are poppyseed, prune, almond, cherry, or cottage cheese.

Polish Tart

1/3 cup butter
3 egg yolks
1/2 cup powdered sugar
1 teaspoon vanilla sugar

1 cup whipping cream
1 cup ground walnuts
30 to 40 ladyfingers
1 cup strong coffee

Topping:
1/2 cup whipping cream
2 teaspoons vanilla extract

fresh fruit, whole walnuts, and/or
    raspberries, optional

Combine butter, egg yolks, sugar, and vanilla sugar. Mix thoroughly until thick and fluffy. Set aside. In a separate bowl beat the whipping cream until stiff.

(continued)

Polish Tart *(continued)*

Fold in the ground walnuts. Gradually add it to the already prepared butter mixture, stirring constantly. Sprinkle ladyfingers with coffee. Coat a large tart pan with aluminum foil. Place ladyfingers on the bottom and along the edges (vertically). Pour half the filling over ladyfingers. Cover with a second layer of ladyfingers; cover with filling. Make two of these layers. The finishing layer will be ladyfingers. Cover with plastic wrap and chill at least 12 hours. Gently turn tart over onto a prepared plate.

Topping: Whip the cream to soft peaks and add the vanilla. Spread over the tart and allow the topping to run down the sides. Garnish with fresh fruit, whole walnuts, or raspberries, if desired.

Walnut Horns

1/3 cup granulated sugar
2/3 cup ground walnuts

1/3 cup butter or margarine
1 1/2 cups flour
1/2 cup powdered sugar

Combine all the ingredients, except powdered sugar, and mix until the mixture is smooth. Put dough into freezer for about 30 minutes. Take 1 tablespoon of dough at a time and roll it in your hands. Put on a greased baking sheet and shape into a horn or crescent. Bake horns at 350° for 10 to 15 minutes. Remove from oven and while they are still warm coat with powdered sugar.

Baked Macaroni with Apples

Maria Ganowska, Chicago, Illinois

4 apples, peeled and shredded
1/2 cup sugar
1 teaspoon cinnamon
1/2 cup raisins, optional

3 cups cooked egg noodles
(homemade optional)
1 tablespoon butter, melted
1/2 cup sour cream

Grease a 9x9-inch pan. Combine apples, sugar, cinnamon, and raisins. Put aside. Place 1/4 of the noodles into the greased pan. Spread 1/4 of the apple mixture over them and sprinkle with melted butter. This is the first layer. Make 3 more layers, sprinkling each with melted butter. Spread sour cream over the top. Bake at 350° for about 45 minutes. Serve hot.

Brandied Peaches

4 peaches, halved, with pits removed   1 cup marmalade or peach preserves
1/2 cup brandy

In a baking dish place peaches round side up. Spoon marmalade or preserves over peaches; sprinkle with brandy. Cover and bake at 350° for 15 minutes.

Cakes

Krakow Region

Cheesecake

1/2 cup raisins
3 tablespoons flour, divided
5 eggs, separated
1/4 teaspoon salt

3 8-ounce packages cream cheese,
  softened
1 cup sugar
1 tablespoon grated lemon peel

Soak raisins in hot water for 15 minutes. Pat dry and coat with 2 tablespoons flour. Preheat oven to 350°. Beat egg whites and salt until stiff. Place egg-white mixture in the freezer for 5 minutes. Combine cheese, sugar, egg yolks and remaining flour; beat until smooth. Stir in raisins and lemon peel. Carefully fold in the egg whites. Pour the mixture into a greased and floured springform pan. Bake for 45 minutes, then turn oven off and leave the cake in the oven until cool.

Apple Cake

2 pounds apples, peeled and cored
1 cup flour
1 cup Cream of Wheat

1 cup sugar
1 teaspoon baking soda
1/2 cup margarine, softened
1 teaspoon vanilla extract

Grease and flour a tart pan. Grate or thinly slice apples. Sift together flour, Cream of Wheat, sugar, and soda; mix well. Blend in margarine. Sprinkle 1/4 of the flour mixture on the bottom of the greased tart pan. Cover with 1/3 of the apples, the next 1/4 of the flour mixture and so on, ending with the flour mixture. Bake at 350° for 1 hour. Before serving it is good to sprinkle cake with the vanilla extract. Serve either hot or cold.

Walnut Torte

8 eggs, separated
1/2 pound sugar
juice and grated rind of 1/2 lemon

20 coffee beans, ground
2 chocolate bars, 3 ounces each, melted
1/2 pound walnuts meats, chopped
1 tablespoon bread crumbs

Filling:

1 cup sweet butter
1 cup sugar
4 chocolate bars, 3 ounces each,
    melted

1 egg yolk
vanilla extract
2 ounces ground almonds

(continued)

Walnut Torte   *(continued)*

Beat egg yolks and sugar together. Add grated lemon rind and juice. Add coffee, melted chocolate, walnuts, and bread crumbs; mix well. Beat egg whites until stiff. Add to torte dough and carefully blend. Divide into three greased 10-inch layer cake pans. Bake at 350° for 30 minutes. While the cake is baking prepare the filling.
Filling: Cream butter and sugar. Add warm melted chocolate, egg yolk, vanilla extract, and almonds. Mix thoroughly. Refrigerate. When the cake is baked and cooled, put the filling on 2 of the layers and top with the third. Garnish with chocolate icing and whole walnuts, if desired.

Dark Cake

3/4 cup butter or margarine
1 1/3 cups sugar
3 tablespoons oil
1/3 cup cold water
1 1/2 tablespoons cocoa

2 cups flour
5 eggs, separated
1 tablespoon baking powder
1 package (5/16-ounce) vanilla sugar
bread crumbs
fresh fruit or nuts, garnish

Melt butter, sugar, oil, water, and cocoa together. Blend and let cool. Add flour, egg yolks, baking powder, and vanilla sugar. Beat egg whites until stiff. Carefully add to mixture. Grease a 12-inch round baking pan. Sprinkle with bread crumbs. Put batter into pan. Bake at 350° for 50 minutes. When cooled, garnish with fresh fruit or nuts.

Sponge Cake

6 eggs, separated
1 teaspoon baking powder
1 1/2 cups sugar

1 1/2 cups flour
1 tablespoon white vinegar
2 tablespoons water

Mix egg yolks together with baking powder. In a separate bowl beat the egg whites until stiff; gradually add sugar. Fold the flour into the beaten egg whites. Fold the yolk mixture into the whites. Add vinegar and water. Bake in a 9-inch round pan for 45 minutes at 350°. Good on its own or as a component for a layer cake.

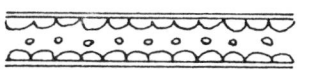

Sponge Layer Cake

1 Sponge Cake recipe (preceding recipe), cut into 3 layers.

Filling:

1 cup sugar, divided
2 egg yolks
1 package (5/16-ounce) vanilla sugar

5 teaspoons powdered milk
1 1/2 cups warm water
1 cup margarine
fresh fruit or nuts

Filling: Beat 1/2 cup sugar and 2 egg yolks together. Combine the remaining sugar, vanilla sugar, powdered milk, and water. Dissolve sugar, then add 4 to 5 teaspoons of the mixture to the egg yolk mixture. Add the egg yolk mixture to the milk mixture. Cream margarine and add the egg yolk mixture. Cover each layer of the sponge cake with the filling and put each layer atop another. Garnish the top layer with fresh fruit or nuts.

Mazurek

1/3 pound butter
4 hard-cooked egg yolks, mashed
1 fresh egg yolk
5 ounces sugar

grated lemon rind
5 ounces almonds, peeled, ground
salt
1/3 pound flour
1 egg, beaten

Cream butter in a large bowl. Add hard-cooked egg yolks, fresh yolk, sugar, lemon rind, almonds, salt, and flour. Mix well. Knead dough for about 5 to 10 minutes. Place dough in freezer for 1 hour. Roll 2/3 of the dough into an 8 1/2x11-inch rectangle. Take the remaining dough and roll it into strands the width of a pencil. Take the long strands and place horizontally and vertically across the rectangle to form many boxes. Brush dough with the beaten egg and bake at 350° for 40 minutes. Cool and put preserves in each box.

Gingerbread

1/3 teaspoon cinnamon
1/2 teaspoon ground cloves
1/2 teaspoon nutmeg
1/4 teaspoon ginger
1/4 teaspoon black pepper
1/4 teaspoon baking powder
1 teaspoon baking soda
1 1/2 cups flour
1 1/2 cups rye flour

1/2 cup butter
1 1/2 cups sugar
1 cup honey
3 eggs, separated
1/2 cup kefir or buttermilk
1/2 cup sour cream
prunes, chopped, optional
figs, chopped, optional
raisins, optional

(continued)

Gingerbread   *(continued)*

Sift together spices, baking powder, baking soda, and flours. In a separate bowl cream butter and sugar; add honey and egg yolks. Add butter mixture to flour mixture. Add kefir and sour cream, mix well. Beat the egg whites until stiff, then fold into dough. If you use the dried fruit, coat it with flour to prevent it from sinking; fold in. Grease and flour a 9x13-inch baking dish. Pour dough into baking dish and bake at 350° for 1 hour.

Note: Should be made ahead of time for a better taste. This is typically baked for Christmas.

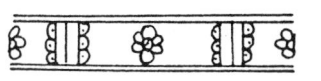

Fruitcake

1 cup butter or margarine
1/2 pound sugar
5 eggs
1/2 pound flour
1 shot glass of vodka or other
   grain alcohol

2 teaspoons baking powder
1 teaspoon vanilla
3/4 cup candied orange skin, chopped
2/3 cup raisins
2/3 cup walnuts, finely chopped
1/2 cup sliced dried figs
1/2 cup pitted dried prunes, diced

Cream butter and sugar, add eggs, flour, alcohol, baking powder and vanilla; blend until smooth. Toss fruit and nuts with enough flour to coat. Add to batter. Place batter in an 11x7x3-inch greased and floured loaf pan. Bake at 350° for 1 hour.

Yeast Cake

1 1/2 ounces yeast
1 tablespoon warm milk
1/4 cup sugar, divided
4 cups flour, divided

2 egg, separated
grated lemon rind
1 teaspoon salt
1 1/2 cups milk
1/4 cup butter, melted

Dissolve yeast in warm milk; add 1 teaspoon of sugar and 1 teaspoon of flour. Beat egg yolks and remaining sugar until light. Put remaining flour into a large bowl. Make a well in the flour. Pour the yeast mixture into well; cover with flour. Wait for the yeast to bubble. If it doesn't, add more yeast. Add egg-yolk mixture, lemon rind, and salt; mix well. Add milk gradually. Knead dough for about 5 minutes and add melted butter, blending it through dough. Put the dough into a greased baking pan and cover. Let rise for 2 to 3 hours. Brush the dough with the egg whites. Bake at 350° for 50 minutes. Test for doneness with a toothpick. If it comes out dry the cake is done.

Poppyseed Cake

Yeast Cake Dough recipe on page 146.

Filling:
3/4 pound poppyseed
1/2 pound sugar
1 tablespoon honey

5 eggs, separated
vanilla extract to taste
1 teaspoon cinnamon or ground cloves
3 ounces almonds, crushed
1 tablespoon flour

Dough: Prepare dough and roll out on a board to fit a jellyroll pan.

Filling: Scald poppyseed and strain in cheese cloth. Grind poppyseed in a blender until smooth. Add sugar, honey, egg yolks, vanilla extract, and cinnamon, blending constantly. Add almonds and blend until well-mixed. Beat egg whites in a separate bowl until stiff. Fold in poppyseed mixture. Sprinkle with flour, mix well. Spread filling over dough and roll as you would a jellyroll. Bake in a large greased loaf pan for 1 hour at 350°. Cool; frost if desired.

Sour Cream Cake

Romie Cierzan, Polish Museum, Winona, Minnesota

1 cup sugar
2 eggs
1 cup sour cream
1/2 teaspoon vanilla

1/4 teaspoon baking soda
1/2 tablespoon water
1 1/2 cups flour
1 1/2 teaspoons baking powder
1/4 teaspoon salt

Beat sugar and eggs together. Add sour cream and vanilla. Dissolve baking soda in water and add to sour cream mixture. Sift together flour, baking powder, and salt. Add to sour cream mixture and beat well. Place in a greased, 9-inch round cake pan. Bake at 375° for 25 to 35 minutes or until done.

Cookies

Easter butter lamb, pisanki, *and* kristka *for doing* pisanki *designs.*

Polish Pecan Cookies

1 cup butter
3 tablespoons vanilla extract
1/2 cup confectioners' sugar

1 1/2 tablespoons water
2 1/2 cups sifted flour
2 cups pecan halves
confectioners' sugar for rolling

Cream butter and vanilla extract; add confectioners' sugar gradually, beating until fluffy. Add water and beat thoroughly. Add flour in fourths, mixing until blended after each addition. If necessary, chill the dough until easy to handle. Shape a teaspoonful of dough around each pecan half, covering nut completely. Place on ungreased cookie sheets. Bake at 400° for 10 minutes. Roll in confectioners' sugar while still warm. Makes about 5 dozen.

Favors

4 egg yolks
1 whole egg
1/2 teaspoon salt
1/3 cup confectioners' sugar

2 tablespoons rum or brandy
1 teaspoon vanilla extract
1 1/4 cups flour
fat for deep frying, heated to 350°
confectioners' sugar or honey, optional

Combine egg yolks, whole egg, and salt in a small bowl of an electric mixer. Beat at highest speed 7 to 10 minutes, until mixture is thick and piles softly. Beat in sugar, a small amount at a time. Then beat in rum and vanilla extract. By hand, fold in flour. Turn onto a generously floured surface.

(continued)

Favors *(continued)*

Knead dough until blisters form, about 10 minutes. Divide dough in half. Cover half of dough with a towel or plastic wrap to prevent drying. Roll out half of dough as thin as possible. Cut dough into 5x2-inch strips. Make a 2-inch slit from center almost to one end of each strip of dough. Then pull opposite end through slit. Repeat with remaining dough. Fry in hot fat until golden brown. Drain on paper towels. If desired, sprinkle with confectioners' sugar or drizzle with honey. Makes 2 1/2 dozen.

Polish Doughnuts

1 package active dry yeast
1/4 cup warm water
1/3 cup butter or margarine, softened
2/3 cup sugar
1 egg
3 egg yolks

1 teaspoon vanilla extract
1 teaspoon grated orange or
  lemon peel
3/4 teaspoon salt
3 1/2 cups flour
fat for deep frying, heated to 375°
confectioners' sugar, optional

Dissolve yeast in warm water. Cream butter and sugar until fluffy. Beat in egg, then egg yolks, one at a time. Add vanilla extract, orange peel, dissolved yeast and salt. Beat until well mixed.

(continued)

Polish Doughnuts   *(continued)*

Stir in flour gradually, adding enough to make a stiff dough. Turn dough onto a floured surface. Knead until smooth and elastic, about 10 minutes. Place in a greased bowl. Cover. Let rise until doubled in bulk. Turn onto lightly floured surface. Pat or roll to 1/2 inch thick. Cut out with a doughnut cutter. Cover. Let rise until doubled in bulk. Fry in hot fat 2 to 3 minutes; turn to brown all sides. Drain doughnuts on paper towels and sprinkle with confectioners' sugar, if desired. Makes about 2 dozen.

Kolacky

1 cup butter or margarine, softened
1 package (8 ounces) cream cheese,
   softened
1/4 teaspoon vanilla extract

2 1/4 cups flour
1/2 teaspoon salt
thick jam or canned fruit filling,
   such as apricot or prune

Cream butter and cream cheese until fluffy. Beat in vanilla extract. Combine flour and salt; add in fourths to butter mixture, blending well after each addition. Chill dough until easy to handle. Roll dough to 3/8 inch thick on a floured surface. Cut out 2-inch circles or other shapes. Place on an ungreased cookie sheet. Make a "thumbprint" about 1/4 inch deep in each. Fill with jam. Bake at 350° for 10 to 15 minutes, or until delicately browned on edges. Makes about 3 1/2 dozen.

Royal Mazurkas

1 cup butter or margarine, softened
1 1/2 cups flour
1 cup sugar
1/4 teaspoon salt

6 egg yolks
1/4 cup ground or finely chopped almonds
1 teaspoon grated orange or lemon peel,
   optional

In a large mixing bowl cream butter until fluffy. Mix flour, sugar, and salt. Alternately beat in 1 egg yolk and a sixth of the flour mixture. Continue until all ingredients are well combined. Stir in almonds and orange peel. Mix well. Roll or pat dough to fit a greased 15x10x1-inch jellyroll pan. Bake at 325° for 35 to 40 minutes or until golden but not browned. Cool in pan on rack 10 minutes. Remove from pan and cut. Makes about 3 dozen.

Mazurkas

1 cup sweet unsalted butter
3/4 cup eggs, beaten
2 cups ground blanched almonds

1 3/4 cups flour
1 cup sugar
1 1/2 cups jam

Cream butter and eggs until fluffy. Mix almonds, flour, and sugar. Add flour mixture, a small amount at a time, to the butter mixture. Beat or knead after each addition. Pat or roll out dough in a greased 15x10x1-inch jellyroll pan. Bake at 350° about 20 minutes or until golden brown. Spread jam over top. Cool for 5 minutes. Cut into 2-inch squares to serve.

Excellent Warsaw Doughnuts

12 egg yolks
1 teaspoon salt
2 packages active dry yeast
1/4 cup warm water
1/3 cup butter or margarine
1/2 cup sugar

4 1/2 cups flour
3 tablespoons rum or brandy
1 cup whipping cream, scalded, divided
1 1/2 cups very thick jam or preserves,
   optional
fat for deep frying, heated to 365°
cinnamon and sugar mix, optional

In a small mixer bowl beat egg yolks with salt at high speed until mixture is thick and piles softly, about 7 minutes. Soften yeast in warm water in a large bowl.

(continued)

Excellent Warsaw Doughnuts   *(continued)*

Cream butter; add sugar gradually, cream until fluffy. Beat into softened yeast. Stir 1/4 of the flour into yeast mixture. Add rum and half the cream. Beat in another 1/4 of the flour. Then beat in egg yolks and rest of cream. Beat 2 minutes. Gradually beat in remaining flour until dough blisters. Cover bowl with plastic wrap. Set in a warm place to rise. When doubled in bulk, punch down. Cover; let dough rise again until doubled. Punch down. Roll dough on a floured board to about 3/4 inch thick. Cut out 3-inch rounds. Use a regular doughnut cutter for plain doughnuts. Use a biscuit cutter for filled doughnuts. To fill doughnuts, place 1 teaspoon of jam in center of half the rounds. Brush edges of rounds with water. Top with remaining rounds. Seal edges. Cover doughnuts on floured surface. Let rise until doubled in bulk, about 20 minutes. Fry doughnuts in hot fat until golden on both sides. Drain on absorbent paper. Sprinkle with cinnamon-sugar, if desired. Makes about 3 dozen.

Rev. Czesław M. Krysa holds a Christmas star-lantern made by Zygmunt Krysa of Lezajsk, Poland.

The lantern is made of paper glued to a wooden frame decorated with "snow" (white tissue paper). The center holds a nativity scene. The center of the star is called swiat *or "the world." Father Krysa is dressed in a traditional Kraków folk costume called a* sukmana *and is wearing a characteristic Polish four-cornered hat called a* rogatywka.